THE
MILLION
DOLLAR
STORY

THE MILLION DOLLAR STORY

An Unexpected Ending

CHRISTINA FERNANDEZ

iUniverse LLC
Bloomington

THE MILLION DOLLAR STORY
AN UNEXPECTED ENDING

iUniverse books may be ordered through booksellers or by contacting:

iUniverse LLC
1663 Liberty Drive
Bloomington, IN 47403
www.iuniverse.com
1-800-Authors (1-800-288-4677)

Because of the dynamic nature of the Internet, any web addresses or links contained in this book may have changed since publication and may no longer be valid. The views expressed in this work are solely those of the author and do not necessarily reflect the views of the publisher, and the publisher hereby disclaims any responsibility for them.

Any people depicted in stock imagery provided by Thinkstock are models, and such images are being used for illustrative purposes only. Certain stock imagery © Thinkstock.

ISBN: 978-1-4917-1696-0 (sc)
ISBN: 978-1-4917-1698-4 (hc)
ISBN: 978-1-4917-1697-7 (e)

Printed in the United States of America.

iUniverse rev. date: 04/14/2014

Characters:

TC: Main character (Female)/narrator. Aggressive type delivers mail but has a passion for basketball which she steered away from being so busy with work

Samantha: TC's girlfriend feminine type, police officer

Jay: TC's guy best friend, real ladies man but has secrets

Crystal: TC's first love beautiful woman tan complexion has a 4 year old

Jenna: TC's side girl that TC kinda likes she likes TC a lot but holds back

Jade: Samantha's side lover aggressive type

Carly: Jay's girlfriend (transvestite)

Susan: Carlys cousin

Moe: Crystal's girlfriend agressive type

John: Moe's/Marly's boyfriends

HOOONNNKKKK . . . BEEP BEEP BEEP . . . .

"Ms. are you ok? Ms.? . . . Hello is this Jay?"

"Yes how may i help you?"

"This is officer Reyes can you tell me who's phone I'm calling you from?"

"TC Tiffany she's a good friend of mine is everything ok with her?"

"I would advise you to meet her at New York hospital she's unconscious."

"Oh my god is she ok what happen?"

"Sir please come to the hospital." (silence)

And although I was unconscious I clearly heard the officer tell my best friend to meet me at the hospital, but what happen? Why was my body so stiff and I could not speak. I felt as though I was having a paralysis dream. I tried and tried to speak but nothing. It all happen about a year ago when I got back in contact with my ex, found out my best friend was ready to come out and most surprising of all the woman of my dreams was cheating on me. This is my story of how I went from the top to the bottom back to the top and right back to the bottom with a whole bunch of drama in between. Please excuse all the random phone calls in between.

TC outside delivering mail

"Hello?"

"Hey Puta was sup, what you doing?"

"Hey Jay, nothing at work was sup with you?"

"I got a hot date tonight and . . ."

"Let me guess you need me to go and double up with you right?"

"Ha yea if you can."

"Yea I got you what time?"

"Let's say around 8ish."

"Ok cool."

Man I never learn my lesson I'm going to go out with this kid and wifey is going to kill me. It's really hot out here lucky thing I'm almost done. You probably wondering who I am, well the name is TC and that was my best friend jay on the phone, I'll explain his story in a few but first a little about me. Well right now I'm 28 years old and I've been delivering mail for a year now. I kind of messed up my career after moving from California to New York. Because I wanted to be with a student, yes a student. It all happened about 10 years ago I graduated high school star basketball player entered college star basketball player with a scholarship. I majored in chemistry and minored in education. I graduated top of my class and was the player of the year all four years. I was offered the opportunity to go pro but I wanted to get my masters so I turned it down. At 22 I started working in a high school teaching a 12th grade class. While I was teaching I played ball every now and then, coached the girls' basketball team and worked on my masters. Oh my goodness this damn phone . . .

"Hello?"

"Hey babe how's work?"

"It's ok I got about 2 hrs to go then I can relax."

"Well that's good timing right?"

"Yea I'm just trying to relax already I'm so tired with all the over time I've been getting. Anyway was sup with you? What you up to?"

"Oh nothing much I got the day off so I'm just cleaning up and I was going to ask if you want me to bring you lunch."

"Sure babe that would be great. Well let me finish up I'll see you in a few . . . love you."

"Ok babie I love you too."

(Clicks phone)

"Hello?"

"Puta, one more thing."

"What?"

"This girl is classy so dress up nice."

"Nigga you know me better then that . . . wifey's bringing me lunch so I'm going to chill with her for a little bit so she won't question me."

"Ok Puta talk to you later."

"Alright bye."

Finally finished this damn route. Now I can go see Jenna till wifey gets here. I haven't seen her in a while so she's going to be surprised. So anyway more about me, I had a lot going for me almost finished with my masters and was making good money had a car my own place and a nice savings account. Then I hit twenty-four and I met the most beautiful woman her name is Samantha. The thing is she was a student of mine but I knew from the day I laid eyes on her I had to have her. It was September ninth I would never forget she was the first student in class she had her hair curled up with a nice tan complexion and her body my goodness proportioned in all the right ways about a 34C boobs and an ass like whoa and I'm a big ass person so I was amazed. Ok let me call this girl I just hope she answers.

"Hello Jenna?"

"Hey ma what you doing? I was just thinking about you."

"Really? I'm outside your building let me in."

"ok! Bye. Bye"

(TC knocks on the door Jenna opens the door and jumps in TC's arms).

"I missed you so much why haven't you been around?"

"Well I've been really busy lately haven't had any free time with the over time I've been getting. So anyway how have you been? You're looking good and what exactly about me were you thinking?"

"I been ok and thanks, I've been hitting the gym a lot, you don't look too bad yourself. And about all the crazy nights we spent together like that day I made you squirt hahahah, So what brings you by today?"

"Hey now we said we would bring that to the grave but it was a good night mmmm a damn good night. Well I finished early and I thought about you so I decided to drop by maybe get another squirting session going."

"Mmm really I like the sound of that."

"Yea but there's only one problem I can't stay long because wifey is meeting me at my job."

"So what you waiting for get over here so I can show you what you've been missing."

Jenna grabs TC and begins to kiss her intimately while caressing her body. The two continue to kiss walking to the bedroom and removing each other's clothing, stopping at the couch TC pushes Jenna onto the couch gets on top of her and starts grinding on her and as Jenna moans TC gets wetter and wetter. TC then begins kissing Jenna on her neck making her way down to her vaginal area putting her fingers inside and stroking slowly while caressing her clit with her thumb. Feeling herself getting close to an orgasm Jenna stops TC and leads her to the bedroom and slams the door behind them.

Samantha's house

"I don't believe you did this shit to my neck! How do you suppose I explain this to TC? In the winter it's fine because I can hide it but what am I going to do now?! This girl is going to have a fit, you're such an asshole!"

"Babie, babie, babie! Relax TC don't give two shits she's probably doing her right now. Here just throw this scarf on and call it a day, it's the style now anyway."

"You always know just what to say; you're the best I swear . . . where have you been all my life?"

"It doesn't matter I'm here now and that's all that counts."

"But Jade babie we have to do something about this, I can't keep doing this what if TC isn't doing anything and I'm here with you, I'm just going to hurt her and she is afraid of that because of previous relationships."

"Babie you're not happy with TC and you know that, you telling me if she wasn't doing her or you didn't suspect anything you wouldn't be here with me right now? You know what don't answer that if you want to stop talking for awhile that's if it's what you really want just be real with me and I will respect whatever it is you want."

"I don't know Jade I mean you do make me happy and I love you but I have to think it over can you give me that and then I can call you tonight. Come on let me take you home so I can be on my way."

"Nah babie its cool I'll just walk, got a lot of thinking to do."

"Ok, I love you."

"Sure you do with every inch of you right? Bye."

"Jade babie please don't act like this not now, give me a kiss."

Jade grabs Samantha and kisses her with so much passion Samantha melts in her arms and Jade gives her a big hug and with tears in her eyes saying I fucking love you Samantha.

"I love you too jade. Ok let's get out of here."

Jade walks home and thinks to herself; man who would have thought I would catch feelings for this girl. This isn't how things were suppose to turn out I'm not sure what I'm going to do but I have to think hard because that time is coming and when it does all hell will break lose.

Jenna's house

"Damn girl did you learn new trick since the last time?"

"No stupid it's just been awhile, you know you the only one I touch. These other 'dykes' don't like to be touched at all."

"Well I'm sorry but this 'dyke' has to get her shit off too."

"And that's why I love this 'dyke'."

Jenna goes to kiss TC. With her hand out TC stops Jenna "hold on my phone, Hello?" (Jenna sucks teeth and walks away).

"TC I'm close to the office, where are you?"

"I just finished the houses I'm going for the pick up now."

"Ok see you in a few."

"Ok bye." (TC hangs up the phone) "Jenna Baby I have to go but I'm going to be doing this route for the rest of the week so I'll be sure to come by."

"Ok T see you later muahz." (Jenna thinks to self) Damn she always does that to me comes by gives me good ass sex and then just leaves. I hate the way I feel for her but I have to play it cool I mean I did get myself in this situation knowing she had wifey and all. Plus I know she stop coming around before because I started getting jealous can't risk that again.

The office area

Look at her man she's fine and after four years she still got it. I don't know why I keep cheating, I have to stop. Things just aren't the same anymore, I mean it's like we are more like friends instead of lovers. She's wearing a scarf must have another hickey on her neck, she thinks I'm stupid. I know she got something with jade but imma let her rock.

"Hey beautiful can I take you out sometime?"

"Ha-ha TC you crazy come here and give me some loving!"

(TC pulls Sam close to her and kisses her cheeks then lips biting then sucking her bottom lip).

"Mmm you better stop before you end up in my house; here I made you mashed potatoes and chicken."

"Really in that case come here, I'm kidding thanks babe you the best."

"I know, ha-ha. So how was your route today? Pretty easy, huh?"

"Yea it was light today no over time or anything; I've been really tired though."

"Yea I know babe I don't know why you came to work in queens. It sucks us not living together anymore, I miss sleeping with you."

"Yea me too babe, hold on a second."

(Sam thinks) I hate that about her I'm trying to have a serious conversation with her and she cuts me off. I'm going to put a stop to this shit.

TC answers the phone

"Hello puta"

"Yea jay was sup"

"I'm going to your house when you get out of work so I can get ready."

"Ok I'm with Sam now so I'll call you later."

"Ok don't cancel on me."

"I'm not nigga, bye"

"So you chillen with Jay again?"

"Yea something like that."

"Hmm ok anyway we need to talk, I've been doing a lot of thinking. I want you to come to my house tomorrow morning."

"Ok no problem, I'll make it happen."

"Well I have to go so I'll see you tomorrow."

"So soon at least wait until I get off, it's only like an hour left."

"Ok fine, so do you like the food?"

"Of course babe it's great, hold on . . . hello?"

"Hey I know you wit wifey but I couldn't stop thinking about you since you left, I want to see you again today."

"Ok I'll give you a call later, bye . . . So babe what you did all day today? Clean your house?"

"Yea but I also did a lot of resting because I've been working long hours."

"Oh ok, that's good you got to rest. Ugh this damn phone, hello?"

"Tiffany?"

"Who's this?"

"You don't recognize my voice? Has it been that long?"

"Crystal? Wow how'd you get my number?"

"Don't worry about that we have to talk, are you busy?"

"Well right now yea, can you give me a call back in like two hours?"

"Yea whatever bye."

"Wow! Thats crazy anyway babe where'd you park lets go sit in your car I got like 45 minutes before I have to clock out."

"Its around the corner come, follow me."

"I'd love to cum hahaha."

"Shut up silly you know what I meant."

"Yea I know."

TC grabs Sam's hand as they walk to the car and when they approach it TC opens the back door directing Sam to sit in the back. TC follows in behind sam and starts kissing her on her cheeks then attempts to kiss her lips and sam moves her head.

"Whats wrong babe?"

"Nothing I'm tired and you not about to fuck me in the backseat of my car in broad day light."

"Really? you have to be kidding me right now, you know what whatever."

TC goes to the front seat and sits with her eyes closed.

"Lets go Im ready to clock out."

(Sam thinking) That was a close one but I'm not about to sit here and let her have her way when she's been giving her phone more attention then me. This has to stop and soon!

Wow what a day anyway where was I, about Sam so she walked in the classroom and all I can think is goddamn she is fine. So she introduces herself as Samantha Cruz and I tell her how ironic that is because my name is tiffany Cruz. So she sits down and we start talking and the rest is history. Four years later and she's wifey and we're happy . . . I think. So how did I end up in NY, well her parents weren't happy with us being together so they told us the only way we can stay together was if after she graduated we moved out of state because they didn't want their family name destroyed. They figured by telling us that we would break up but instead her at eighteen and me at twenty-five moved to NY with one of my sisters. It was hard finding a job so I went toward the easiest thing teacher's assistant and Sam joined the police academy and became a police officer in the Bronx. The job I had wasn't paying enough so I got a job in queens delivering mail which caused me to move out here.

"Ok I'm done lets be out this place. Are you coming to my house or going home?"

"I'm just going to go home I still got a few things to do."

"Of course you do call me later, when you get home . . . I love you"

"I love you too bye"

(Sam in her car crying) I don't know what happen to us we are so far apart right now, she always insisted on being around me and now it's like fuck it if we chill we chill if we don't oh well and little does she know I'm about to end this madness.

So ever since I got this job I've been away from Sam because she decided to keep the apartment we shared in the Bronx since she had the job as a police officer. Ever since we've been living in separate apartments we've really grown apart. I started to do me and she's been hanging with this jade girl that she met in the academy. She tells me they hang as friends and go over police stuff sometimes but I know otherwise. Now my boy Jay I met this dude at the teacher's assistant job in the school where I worked, he's the coach and we became instant friends. The first time we chilled outside of work . . . ugh this phone

"Hello?"

"Puta I'm on my way to your house, ok?

"Cool so am I, see you there."

"Hello?"

"Tiffany!"

"Crystal?"

"Yea it's me are you still busy?"

"Not really, I'm on my way home from work was sup?"

"Well I don't want to talk over the phone so when and where can we meet?"

"Well you can come to my house now if you want I live in Queens on the A line."

"Ok what's your address?"

"It's 10927 97 street."

"Hmm ok I'll be there in a few, ok?"

"Ok I'll be here."

That was crystal my first love spent four years with that girl, man I really miss those days but back to Jay. So he was telling me how he met this real pretty girl about a week before who had a cousin that just moved to queens and he wanted to date the girl but he needed someone to take her cousin out and he would have invited his brother but the cousin is gay. So I told him I would go because it was time for me to meet new people anyway. So he told me to be by his house around nine. I said ok went home threw on my favorite blue jeans a red button up and a fresh pair of shoes, and was on my way to his house. The wife had overtime so I didn't have to worry about any arguments. I got to jay's place around 9:15 and when I walked in his apartment there were two fine women sitting in the living room. So he introduced me as TC and he introduced the ladies Tasha who was his date and Jenna who was my date.

(Knocks on door)

"Who is it!?"

"It's me open up"

(TC opens the door) "My goodness wow crystal you look good."

"Thanks you don't look too bad yourself.

(TC stuck in a daze)

"So you going to be rude and just let me stand here?"

"No, no come in would you like something to drink?"

"Yes, some water would be nice."

"Ok just sit here in the living room. So was sup, what gives me the pleasure of having you in my living room?"

"Well it's been about seven years and I thought we had a lot of catching up to do especially since you been in NY for the past couple of years."

"That's cool I guess, I mean we can definitely get up sometime but not tonight. I got something to take care of."

(Knock on door)

"Hold on a sec. I'm coming!" (TC opens the door to see her best friend standing there) Was sup Jay?"

"T my main girl, was sup when you gonna start getting ready?"

"Go ahead and shower up, I already got my clothes ready just need to shower and get dressed. (Whispers) Remember that girl I always told you about, my first love? She's here in the living room, come let me introduce you. Crystal this is my boy Jay, Jay Crystal."

"Hello Crystal, nice to meet you. Heard a lot about you."

"Well it's nice to meet you Jay, and tell me was what you heard good or bad?"

"Not too bad you're an ok girl; sorry things didn't work for the two of you."

"Yea I guess but you live and you learn then correct your mistakes."

"Yea that's true well it's nice meeting you but I got to go shower."

"Ok honey. So TC what's up with you? How's NY treating you?"

"Well I've been here three years now; worked in a school in the Bronx for a little bit now I'm in Queens delivering mail and playing ball for money."

"That's nice, as for me ever since we broke up I came to NY on a scholarship to Fordham University graduated there got my masters and now I'm teaching at the University. In college I met a guy vardly and we went together for my entire undergrad time. I had a baby boy who is four now and very smart."

"Wow, so how's the love life now?"

"Well I have a girlfriend met her when JR. was two and we been together since. Lately things seem to be going down I don't know why, seems like we are fading apart."

"Wow that's crazy, and as much as I hate to end like this I have to go shower and get ready. You can stay until we leave if you want."

"Yea sure that will be fine but I have to get my son before I go home."

"Ok that's not a problem."

Wow Crystal is here and after so long, has me wondering why she really came to see me. I mean things were really bad between us so why would she want to have anything to do with me? What happened with us is any person's next question. Well we met in high school, junior year for me and sophomore year for her. I was the star of the girls' basketball team and she was just Crystal. I was faithful to her to the best of my ability but because of her insecurities she kept accusing me of messing around with every girl I talked to, so I stopped talking to all my friends. She also went to every game I had whether it was home or away. It was crazy I couldn't even talk on the phone at one point without it being on speaker. I loved her so much that I didn't care to do whatever it took for us to be together. After I graduated high school she was still a senior and being that I had a car I would pick her up from time to time. I still had school, basketball and work so it was getting unbearable. Eventually I told her we should see other people and she said ok but that wasn't what she really wanted and of course she didn't say anything. She ended up doing crazy shit like starving herself, not going to school and being hospitalized like once a week. Being that I did love and care for her I was always there and she ended up telling me that she didn't want to lose me and I told her I felt the same but she had to stop her insecure ways. So we got back together eventually. Just to give a little background on crystal, she's a very beautiful girl but all her relationships before me went really bad. She got played, was physically, mentally and emotionally abused all before the age of sixteen. On top of all that she was molested by her mother's brother who really played a part on her insecurities. I remember the day she told me the story, she had me to tears wanting to kill that man and her mother. One day we sat in my room and we were arguing about her insecurities and she sat me down looked me in my eyes and said:

"Do you want to know why I'm so insecure? Let me tell you, because I'm ugly and dirty inside and out I have no morals."

"No."

"Let me finish! Everything in my life is disastrous."

"Ok."

"When I was thirteen years old I got home from school a little late but there was still a bunch of people in my house my mother's brother being one of them. Being that I don't get along with people too much and I like to be alone I just went to my room and started my homework. So the bastard comes in my room and locks the door but I don't think anything of it so I continue my work. He then leans over me and says; 'Mmm you smell so good; I would love to taste you.' So I ask him to get out of my room but he ignores me and turns my radio up really loud. Then he grabs me throws me on the bed telling me not to worry it's going to be ok and that I'm going to enjoy myself. So I start kicking, screaming and even biting but he didn't stop. Instead he leaned over and said; 'Keep on baby I like it rough.' I then stood still and by then he was done he got up opened the door and went to the living room. I followed behind him and attempted to tell my mom as I told her she slapped me and said; 'how dare you lie on my brother like that?' I left the house and cried every night since. Then I find you and you're everything but because of what happened to me I can't find myself to trust anyone again and I can't control my feelings. I love you with all my heart and I'm sorry for making things hard, I'm just scared to lose you because you're all I got."

Then I told her that I loved her too and that I would always be there for her. So we got back together and things were going pretty good. She was focused in school, had an after school job and was planning to attend college. Me I was in my first year of college, playing basketball and working. I ended up being real busy and she started accusing me again, so instead of leaving her I fed into it and started doing me making sure everyone knew she was wifey. So things stood that way until she finished high school, she decided to take a year off school before she went to college, quit her job and insisted on moving in with me and I said ok, for what was that . . . (Knocks on door):

"Yo TC what the fuck, how long you going to be in there?"

"Oh damn I lost track of time, I'm getting out now. Crystal! Come over to my room I have to show you something. Look this is my master bedroom has a bathroom and a walk-in closet, you like it?"

(Crystal thinking) My goodness she is so sexy and that body my god I would love to have my way with her right now.

"Do you like my room?"

"Oh yes, it's beautiful. (Whispers) Like you."

"Thanks I decorated it myself. And what you said under your breath?"

"That's good, well I got to get going so I'll give you a call so we can chill, and nothing."

"Oh ok, where you headed?"

"I have to go to the Bronx, that's where I live."

"Really, how are you getting there?"

"Probably a cab but, most likely the train."

"Oh damn, we going to the Bronx also. You want a ride?"

"Yea sure I'll take the ride."

"Ok let me get dressed."

"Yo, T hurry up! I still gotta get these girls."

"Ok I'm coming!

So getting back to me being introduced to Jenna. When I laid my eyes on that girl I was so impressed because I didn't think Jay had good taste in woman but my goodness she was fine. She had long black curly hair, a fat ass and a nice body structure. She walked up to me about five feet and she spoke with the sweetest voice causing my stomach to turn with pleasure. From that moment I knew I was in trouble because I was going to cheat on Sam for the first time. The last time I cheated I was with Crystal and it wasn't a good feeling in the end. So the four of us went to a restaurant then to the movies. So as we are on the date Jenna and I are getting along smoothly. Jay realizes the chemistry and he made a stupid comment about someone falling in-love meaning me. So here I go with my big mouth "what nigga you crazy if anything it's the other way around. You must not know about me, I get girls easy." So he doubts me highly so I just tell him that I'm going to show him a little something. I hit it off with Jenna for the rest of the night and I was being charming because I now had a point to prove. (Knock on door)

"T hurry up man!"

"Ok pato I'm ready, let's go."

(Jay, TC, and Crystal are in Jay's car going to pick up Carly. Crystal and TC are in the back seat.)

"Damn girl you looking real good, not saying you didn't always but damn."

"Shut up Tiffany, you so stupid."

"How bout we stop calling me Tiffany and start calling me TC, how about that."

"Oh hell no! Not talking to me like that, you know damn well I always call you Tiffany."

"Excuse me guys I hate to interrupt but this is Carly. Carly, TC and Crystal."

"Hi, nice to meet you."

"Same."

"OOOk now that that's done, Crystal where to?"

"You can just drop me off on Gun hill near the two train, I can take it from there."

"Ok, no problem."

(TC and Crystal are in the back seat playing around real touchy feely)

"Tiffany stop you play too much."

"What happen you don't want to catch feelings?"

"Yea right I am so over that, I got some new tricks now and catching feelings isn't one of them."

"Really that's good to know means I have to work extra hard and go to the closet and pull some tricks from there."

"I guess if that's how you feel."

"I hate to interrupt you love birds but we here."

"Ok thanks for the ride."

"T I'll call you later."

"Let me walk you out, so where you headed now?"

"Imma go get my son then I'm going home."

"Ok cool so call me later tonight."

(TC opens arms asking for a hug the two hug with true compassion for one another).

(Jay and Carly chat while TC talks to Crystal)

"So what's up ma how you been? You real quiet."

"I'm ok just observing a lil something, my day was cool went to work had an ok day then went home and got some rest."

"Oh so you got a good rest cause you know we were going out tonight, right?"

"Yea I got a lot in store for you tonight hint, hint, wink, wink."

"Haha you so crazy got me blushing and shit."

"Wow, do I really that's a good thing. I don't mean to get off topic but TC is single, right?"

"Oh yea, yea that's an old ex she was with in California."

"Oh ok looks like they got something going."

"Oh no she's single."

"Ok, I just don't want my cousin getting into any drama or anything."

"Yea I feel you."

(TC gets back in the car with a big smile)

"Damn nigga you look like you in-love."

"Chill Jay watch your mouth, that's over."

(Jay, Carly and TC pickup Carly's cousin Susan) So back to Jenna that night I didn't go too far to impress being that I didn't want to seem like a beast. The night was over and because she lived in Queens and we were in the Bronx I took the train with her, yes the train a lil trick I use to get to know the ladies and spend QT. So we on the train and she's telling me about herself and she seems to like all the things I like and I tend to catch myself being impressed. So I tell myself fall back don't let her grasp any feelings cause then shit is going to hit the fan. So finally we reach her stop get off the train and walk to her house, we talk in front of her door for 5 minutes then I get a call

"Hello?" Hey babe wassup? Ok no problem, ok bye."

"Babe?"

"You never asked but yea I got wifey been with her for a lil minute now and you are actually the first girl I been out with since I got with her. So you should consider yourself lucky."

"Oh really you must not know who you talking to, I'm one of kind and have the ability to get what I want when I want, you dig?"

"Ok now, you sound real confident but you know what I'm going to let you rock."

"I got to head home so I'm leaving now, talk to you later."

"Ok cool."

(TC moves in on Jenna to get a hug and attempts a kiss on her lips; Jenna hugs TC and moves her face giving TC her cheek).

I walk down the block and hop in a cab, Jenna calls but I ignore it.

"T we here go to that house right there her name is Susan."

"No man I don't know her."

"I'll get her." (Carla steps out the car)

"T are you ok you killing me here man."

"Killing you? I'm killing myself ever since Crystal came by I can't seem to get her off my mind and its driving me crazy."

"Oh damn man she's sparking you up, huh?"

"Yea man I don't know what it is but since I saw her I felt the same way from when we were together, I'm in love with her man there's no question about that."

"Wow man we got to talk you want to talk now?"

"Nah man we can talk another day lets enjoy our night."

"Aight cool."

(Carly goes to the house to get Susan) "Hey girl wassup you ready?"

"Yea just give me a minute."

"Ok take your time I got to give you the info on this TC character."

"Oh really let me have it."

"Well for starters she is very pretty and has a way with words but don't let her laid back mentality fool you, she's a player and she knows what she doing. She has the ability to make women fall for her if they let down their guard."

"That's why you my favorite cousin cause you always looking out."

"Well you know me now bring your ass on. Let's go. Jay, TC this is my cousin Susan."

"Hello guys nice to meet you."

"Nice meet you too."

"Ok, so for starters we going out to get something to eat, then we going to hit a comedy club and after that we can take things from there."

(The four are driving to get some food TC and Susan are in the back and Jay and Carly are talking in the front. TC is really quiet during the ride.)

I know I was talking about Jenna but ever since I saw Crystal I can't stop thinking about her so I'm going to continue the story about her Ok so I was talking about us moving in together. When we first moved in things were great, I was going to school and working and she just graduated and just left her job. I would go to school early in the morning, had basketball practice then had to be at work, so I was busy most of the day I would leave at 9A.M. and be home sometimes by 11P.M. Mind you when we moved in together I dropped all the females I was messing with because I really did want to be with her. So yea the first year was really good but about a year and a half later shit started going downhill, she started going through my things while I was out, calling me every hour and worse of all we weren't having sex. So for example one day I got up as quiet as possible not to wake her made breakfast for the both of us woke her up gave her the plate we ate together then I got ready for school and I'm on the phone with a teammate talking about a game that we have so she walks in the bathroom flipping because I'm on the phone. Asking who I'm on the phone with and why so I tell my teammate to hold on and I explain it to her but she wasn't trying to hear it. I told my teammate I was going to call her later and got off the phone. For what was that Crystal just flipped saying I was hiding something and that she was done she didn't want to be with me. So to avoid a fight I left without a word. From that day on I didn't see or speak to her until today but never forgot about her.

"TC honey we here."

"Oh damn did I fall asleep?"

"Ha-ha yea you kind of did, but its ok."

(The four walk into the restaurant and being polite as always TC opens doors for Susan and saying pleasant things to her.)

"T what are you going to get?"

"Honestly I have no clue. I was thinking maybe something with a pork chop. What you trying to get."

"I don't know but I want some steak." What about you ladies, you got anything in mind?"

"I don't know about Susan but I want some pasta."

"I think I want some pasta too."

"Ok well now that we all know what we want lets order."

The four eat their individual meals while laughing and joking at the table. Once everyone is done they all get up and walk to the car.

"So Susan, did you enjoy your meal?"

"Yes TC I actually did. Did you?"

"It was ok but talking to you was a lot better."

"Really, I'm glad you feel that way. You really are charming; one couldn't help but like you."

"Ha-ha no need to say it like that, but yea I make it my business to show everyone I meet a good time."

"Yea I noticed but I have to go home now so I guess we can meet up another time."

"Ok no problem, would you like me to take you home?"

"Oh no its fine I'll go alone. Thanks though."

"Ok cool so I guess you can get my number from your cousin whenever you ready to call me."

"Yea I guess. Goodnight."

(The two hug and kiss goodnight. TC walks toward Jay and Carly).

"Jay I'm going to Samantha's so I catch up with you later."

"Ok cool but come here for a second I have to talk to you for a minute."

"What's up?"

"Hey I think this girl may be the one for me but something is fishy about her. I mean she's great in every way but she won't have sex with me. I mean every type of sex except regular sex."

"Hmm, know what I'm thinking?" She might be a dude."

"That's the same shit I was thinking but I don't know man. I'm kind of happy and if she is I don't know what I will do."

"Well you know what I would say about that but it's up to you bro."

"Alright let me get out of here."

While Jay and TC talk, Susan and Carly also talk.

"So what do you think of TC?"

"Yes she is charming and my goodness she is fine."

"Told you, but you didn't fall, did you?"

"No, I kept it short and to the point. What about you? What you going to do about Jay?"

"I don't know, like I want to tell him how I feel and everything but I'm scared he's going to fall back if I tell him."

"Well you are going to have to tell him one day. You can't keep it a secret forever."

"Yea I know I'll say something eventually just let me get a little more comfortable."

"Ok cuzo I love you, I have to get going good luck with that."

"I love you too, thanks for coming through for me. I'll call you when I'm home."

(Jay and Carly go in Jay's car. TC gets in a cab to Samantha's house and Susan walks home thinking about a lot of things).

(Susan thinking) wow what an experience and man my cousin is good. I don't know how she pulls that shit off. That TC girl is cute and her swag is crazy but I have to fall back I have wifey just didn't want Carly to go out alone.

(TC is sitting in the cab on her way to Samantha's house).

Wow that Susan kind of got me thinking but it's whatever I got more important things to consider. Like my situation with Samantha and the return of Crystal I don't know how I'm going to handle all this. Well I'm on my way to see Sam now she isn't expecting me so she should be really glad to see me. So anyway more about Jenna, so she calls me but I'm like nah I'm not going to answer she's too full of herself. So like a week later she calls me again and I'm at work so she invites me over to her house. So I finish work as fast as I can and I head to her place and when I get there I'm fascinated by her appearance. I thought she looked good the day I met her but she had me fooled she looked extra good when I got to her house. So I walk in and she shows me around making the bedroom the last stop she tells me to sit on the bed and give her a minute to get something from the kitchen at the same time she asks if I want anything. I ask for a cup of juice and wait till she gets back. She brings me a cup full of juice and she sits next to me turning on the radio. We sit there and chat for a little while then she gets closer to me allowing me to smell her aroma and when I say it was good man it was good. That smell had me so open I had no choice but to kiss her so we began kissing and one thing lead to another. Next thing you know it's 3:50 and I have to be to work by 4:00 so now I'm rushing to get out of there of course I made it back. From that day on me and Jenna have been kicking it hard till one day that all fell off. That I'll get into another time.

(TC gets out the cab and walks to Samantha's house. Knocking on the door she gets a phone call).

"Hello?"

"Tiffany we have to talk what you doing?"

"Well I can't talk right now; I just got to wifeys house."

"Hmm ok I guess."

(TC knocks on Sam's door and Samantha opens the door with a confused look on her face).

"Hey babe, what are you doing here?"

"What am I doing here? Damn thought you would be happy to see me. Seems like you disappointed."

"Oh no baby it's surprising to see you here being that you hardly ever visit me."

"Well I was thinking it's time for a change and that me and my wife should spend a lot more time together. What do you think about that?"

"What do I think? It would be a pleasure about time I see you more. Babe give me one second I have to do something before you come in."

Yea she got someone in there but I'm not going to sweat her I'll catch her one of these days. This is unfortunate that things are going to end, I really love this girl. This Crystal girl coming back isn't making things easy at all well here we go.

"Ok babe come in."

"So what were you doing?"

"Huh?"

"I asked what were you doing being that you had me waiting outside for like ten minutes."

"Oh I wanted to clean up a little bit being that I wasn't expecting you, I had a little mess going on."

"Hmm ok good one. Anyway can you give me something to drink I'm thirsty."

"What the hell is that supposed to mean, good one? You think I'm lying or something?"

"I don't want to get into it just get me something to drink."

"You know what it's whatever."

(Samantha walks to the kitchen and her phone rings).

"Hello?"

"Hey babe that was a close one, what are you doing?"

"Yea it was; I'm not doing anything. I'm going to call you back in a few."

"Hmm, ok."

(Samantha walks back to the bedroom where TC is sitting on the bed watching TV).

"Here's your water."

"I'm not really liking the vibe I'm getting from you right now. Did I come at a bad time or is there something you want to tell me?"

"TC baby you know I love you with all my heart but things aren't the same. I mean we don't spend any time together and when we do it's like ten or twenty minutes and this isn't how I want to be in a relationship."

"So are you telling me you don't want to be with me anymore?"

"Honestly baby I don't know what I want; maybe we should take some time off and see other people. Just to see how things play."

"Wow ok umm I don't really know what to say, I guess I'll just go home. Goodnight Sam, I love you."

"Goodnight T. I love you too baby."

(TC leaves Sam's place confused not realizing what really happened).

Man how did I know this was going to happen. Shit! What is happening and why didn't I stay and talk things out with her. I don't know what to think, how to feel wow this is crazy. AAAAHHHHH WHAT THE FUCK!! I don't believe this is happening I can't lose this girl what would I do without her? I have to think things over like what is going to happen? How do I deal with Samantha not wanting me and Crystal's return? I'm just going to go home and get some sleep.

(TC gets in a cab and cries the whole ride home. When she finally gets home she takes a shower puts her phone on silent and goes to sleep).

Samantha's house

(Samantha is pacing back and forth in her hallway with tears flowing from her eyes as she thinks about what she just told TC).

(Samantha thinking out loud) I don't believe I just told her that but no wait fuck that how she just left like that. OMG I just lost my fucking wife, best friend, baby, my everything and for a girl who probably isn't even worth the shit. I have to call her but no if I call her she won't take me seriously. And now my phone is ringing none stop but it isn't who I want it to be aye whatever.

"Hello?"

"Babe I'm calling to tell you I'm going to sleep now."

"You calling me to tell me you going to sleep are you serious? You couldn't come up with something better than that? You want to know what happen, I fucking told her we should see other people and now she's gone but I don't know if this is what I want. I'm going to sleep now don't say anything I'll talk to you in the morning. Goodnight."

"Hello? Sam? Wow she just hung up on me. Whatever I'm done."

Jade's house

"This is getting out of hand I hope you know what you doing. I mean I'm starting to catch feelings for this girl so you better do something quick because I can't do this anymore."

"Don't worry I'm almost in there just give me like another week."

"Ok sis one week that's it."

"Ok damn stop being a pussy."

Jay's house

(Jay and Carly are lying in the bed Carly on Jay's chest).

"Damn baby you sure know how to put in work."

"You already know, I've wanted to do that to you for a long time now."

"Well I'm glad I got it sooner than later ha-ha. But I have to ask; why do you leave out the missionary position?"

"About that, I was waiting for the perfect time to tell you this but I guess there is no perfect time so . . ."

"So?"

"Well . . . . umm I don't know how you going to feel about this but I'm . . ."

"You're what? Come on let me have it already!"

"I'm gay."

"That's it you're gay? Ok that isn't bad, you gay and you like me so what. I can handle this."

"No you don't understand."

"Huh? What don't I understand?"

"Ok honey, I'm gay and I . . ."

"You what?"

TC's house

Oh man look at the time, I have to call Sam.

"Hello, babe?"

"TC?"

"Yea it's me, what are you doing?"

"I'm home cleaning, why are you calling me?"

"We have to talk babe, can I go over?"

"Umm sure whenever you're ready."

"Ok I have to shower then I'm going to go."

"Ok, bye."

"Babe!"

"Yes?"

"I love you."

"I love you too, bye."

"See you in a few."

Ok so she still wants to talk to me this is great I have to think of something not to lose this girl. But what about Crystal? What the hell is my problem she's old news Sam is here now and she's a great woman and I don't want to lose that. What if she found out I've been cheating and what if she's fed up with my shit? Man I just dug a deep hole for myself damn.

Samantha's house

So TC thinks she's going to come over here and patch things up but I can't let that be I have to be strong. One month is all I need but I really like Jade what if after a month I really don't want TC anymore. This isn't as easy as I thought it would be.

(TC driving to Samantha's house).

So on the way to Sam's let me continue on Jenna well we chilled hard for a while but then she started getting jealous and calling me all hours of the night asking who I was with. I wasn't feeling her actions and wifey was beginning to question it so I stopped talking to Jenna for a while. The other day was the first time I saw her in months but if Sam takes me back today I'm cutting off all the girls. Not like there's many but the few that there are. Well here we go hopefully I get good news.

(TC knocks on Sam's door; Sam opens and lets her in.)

"So about last night, what was that about and are you serious?"

"Yes I am serious and it's about the fact that I don't want to be in something that doesn't really exist."

"Doesn't really exist? What's that suppose to mean?"

"Come on now babe, we both know things aren't good between us. We hardly talk to one another it's a miracle if we see each other and I can count on one hand how many times we had sex this month."

"So that's what it's about? You want more sex I'll give you more sex."

"See babe you got it all mixed up, it isn't about the sex it's about the connection. It's gone; we are not on the same level anymore."

"Babe please just tell me what you want and I'll do it you can't just end like this."

"I just need some time, to think things through. Let's just do our own thing for a little while and see where things go and how we feel."

"Man I don't even know what to say but because I love you I'm going to have to respect how you feel."

"Thank you."

"Yup, I have to run."

"Ok I guess we can talk later, bye T."

"Bye Sam."

(TC leaves Sam's place and gets in her car).

Man this is crazy, what is there to do now? Five years down the drain for some stupid shit that could have been worked out if the reasons she's giving me are true. I would never have thought things would end like this, maybe she does just need some time.

"Hello?"

"Tiffany? You ok?"

"Yea, I'm good Crystal what's up?"

"Well I called you yesterday to see if you had time to talk and you didn't so I decided to call today and see if you have a few minutes."

"Honestly not right now give me a few hours and call me back."

"Oh ok cool."

This girl is really starting to urk me but maybe it's just because I'm hurting right now. I honestly don't know what to do this is crazy.

Jay's house

"Ok you're gay and you what."

"Ok I'm gay and I like men."

"I'm confused, are you telling me you're a man?"

". . . . yes I am. And I understand if you're mad and you never want to see me again but I really do like you. This is why I took so long to tell you."

"So that's what you do? Wait till the person really likes you to tell them you're a man?"

"No that's the thing at first I thought you knew. Because when we met it was in a gay club and all."

"Well I go to gay clubs with my friend who is gay but I don't try to bag anything and when you came up to me I was skeptical but you didn't look . . . .

"I'm so."

"You didn't look like a man! This could really ruin my reputation, how do you suppose I tell my family? And to think I was going to bring you to my parents house this weekend."

"I'm sorry baby and I know I should have been told you but the first day we chilled I had so much fun I didn't want to ruin it and I was going to tell you but things just got better."

"You know what's really crazy? I don't even know what to do. I spoke to TC the other day and we suspected it but I was hoping otherwise because I'm really happy with you."

"I'm happy with you too baby and this is why I couldn't say anything but I won't force you to be with me I will leave the decision up to you. Just know I really do like you and want to be with you."

"I have to think about this, let me take you home for now."

"No babe its fine I'll take a cab."

"Ok let me call one then."

"No its fine I can handle it."

"Ok, I guess. Goodnight, call me when you get home."

"Ok I will."

Man I got what I expected how am I suppose to deal with this? I have to call TC and tell her crazy ass, she probably hoped it on me or some shit. (Jay picks up the phone and calls TC but gets on answer) T when you get this call me you not going to believe what just happened to me. Well maybe you will but whatever just call me. Well I got a lot of thinking to do I'm about to hit this shower and go to bed.

Let's see what all these damn voicemails are about. Ok Crystal delete, Crystal delete, Crystal again damn delete and my boy Jay, I have to go check this kid. (TC calls Jay).

"Hello T, damn girl where you been I've been calling you."

"Yea I know man I'm sorry I just left Sam's place. I'm going to your house we have to talk."

"You in the Bronx damn nigga ok I'll be here."

"Ok I'm going to grab something to eat, you want something?"

"Nah I'm good just hurry up because I got some shit for you too."

"Ha-ha iight I'll be there in like ten."

"Ok."

So all the stories are up to date Crystal, Sam and Jenna. That's it with the girls I mean there were a few in between but those were the main ones Crystal the first, Sam the wife and Jenna the down low chick that keeps me going back for more every now and then. What's going to happen now I wish I knew but all I know is I have to try my best with Sam but at the Same time let go cause I don't want to feel what I felt with Crystal. Now my boy Jay's story, he's a good person and very caring but he has issues that go back to when he was a kid. He never met his dad and his stepdad was the biggest dick you will ever meet. He used to beat Jay's mom and treated Jay like a stranger. When Jay got to high school he played ball and did his thing, could have had any girl he wanted but there was one person he had his eye on but because of his pride and not wanting to get teased he never approached the person and they never knew. Jay was into this really cool gay dude that was always around the team but he never got to experience it so instead he was with multiple girls but always unhappy. He ended up falling for this one girl but she treated him like shit always disrespected him in front of his friends, was with a bunch of dudes and brought guys around Jay's hood. For awhile Jay put up with it till he couldn't take it anymore and he moved from Queens to the Bronx and haven't seen his High School love since. Jay is real insecure because of how he feels for guys but his pride won't let him open up but when he met me all that changed. When we first met he was real cocky and confident with his but after awhile he started opening up to me so I decided to take him with me to gay clubs and though he was comfortable he never tried to get with anyone till the one day we went and he met Carly. I knew she was a man but he made himself believe she wasn't so I went along with it figuring he probably knew but didn't want to face it. Since the girl from High School Jay has been real careful and cold with women to avoid getting hurt but I realize he is opening up with Carly and he seems real comfortable so I'm happy for him.

(TC knocks on Jay's door and he lets her in).

"It took you long enough; did you make the food yourself?"

"No asshole there was traffic and Sam doesn't live that close to you."

"Ok relax I was joking, so am I starting or are you."

"Well most likely your situation is better than mine so I'll start. So I go to Sam's yesterday and when I get there she looks surprised but not surprised like happy to see me more like oh what the fuck I'm caught. So whatever she stops me at the door and leaves me outside for like ten minutes then lets me in."

"So you think she had the next bitch in the house which she probably did but go ahead."

"Yea let me finish. So anyway I tell her how I'm not feeling the negative energy and I asked if she had something to tell me and to make a long story short she broke up with me."

"Wow T I'm sorry to hear that are you ok?"

"Well I went to see her again today and she said she needs time, so basically I guess I have to start moving on."

"What if she comes back though?"

"Shit happens, I'm not going to sit and wait for a heart break. I mean if it's meant to be then when and if she comes back I will be willing to be with her . . . right?"

"I don't know man, only God can answer that."

"Yea I know but anyway what's your news."

"Well it's about Carly, she's a man."

"Ok and. What are you going to do?"

"Well I put up a front like I was shocked but we both know I knew, I'm just scared. How would I tell my family? What about kids? I do want some one day."

"Jay baby you got me here to support you and just because you are gay doesn't mean you can't have children. You can always find a girl to help you out or adopt. About your family well I met your mom and your stepdad you don't have to worry about what he thinks he's a dick anyway. Hey man I'm your friend and if no one else will support you I'm here fuck everyone else. Now give me a hug."

(Jay goes in to hug TC)

"Thanks T baby you the best, I think I should call Carly now."

"Yea you do that and I'm going to call Crystal and see what she been blowing me up for."

"Ha-ha, maybe she wants you back."

"Yea whatever get out of here . . . Hello, Crystal?"

"Hey TC what are you doing?"

"Oh nothing in Jay's house thinking whether we going out to eat or if I'm going to make him cook for me."

"AAAAHHHH I think you should go out that way I can go and we can do some catching up."

"That sounds like a good idea let me see what Jay wants to do and I'll give you a call back."

"Ok cool not a problem."

(Jay is in his bedroom on the phone with Carly).

"Hello?"

"Hey Jay baby I didn't think you would ever call me back."

"Well I was thinking and I spoke to TC about you and I realized that you make me happy. I mean I haven't been this happy since my high school days when I was crushing on this one du . . . . I mean girl for awhile. So I guess what I'm trying to say is I want to see how things go and I want to make things between us work."

"Omg babe I'm so happy you came around. I didn't think this was going to happen but I'm really happy. We have to celebrate, let's go out to eat."

"Yes that sounds great, I'll pick you up around eight-ish."

"Ok baby see you then, bye."

"Bye."

"So I guess things went well."

"Yea she I mean he wants to go out to eat. Are you coming?"

"Yea Crystal wants to chill so we can all go like a double date."

"AAAHHH; yea that's great so where we going?"

"I don't know but I have to call Crystal and let her know. Is eight good?"

"Yea that's fine."

"Hello."

"Yea I spoke to Jay we should be there by eight something so be ready by like eight."

"Ok will do."

"Ok, bye."

"Later."

(Crystal is in her house with her girlfriend and Jade).

"Jade baby I did it."

"Did what?"

"Today is the big day. I set up a date with TC so now all I need you to do is call this Samantha girl and invite her out to chill. As soon as I find out where we going I will let you know so you can take her there."

"Ok Crystal this better work because after today I'm done. What about Moe?"

"Please girl Moe aint worried about me, she's too busy on that damn game. Plus she's staying with the baby."

"Iight Crystal whatever I'll call Sam now."

"Hello Sam baby don't hang up."

"Ok Jade I'm listening what you have to tell me?"

"Well I don't know about you but I thought you leaving T was going to be a good thing for us. I'm happy we can actually be now and stop sneaking around. To show my appreciation of you making such a big sacrifice I was wondering if you let me take you out."

"Wow Jade just when I think of leaving you alone you do and say the sweetest things. Sure we can go out. I have to get ready though so give me some time."

"Its fine babe take all the time you need."

"Ok I'll call you when I'm ready."

"Ok talk to you later."

"Damn Jade you got some serious game I should have had my notebook out for that one."

"Please Crystal I really do like her and if things go good for you and T then I'm going to try and stay with Sam. She's a good girl."

"Yea lil sis but you left out one thing. She's a cheater."

"Please she wasn't happy when I met her."

"So that makes it right? What if you two become an item and another you comes along? Then what?"

"I don't know but all I know is that I like her and I'm willing to take that chance. Shit that's what life is about right? Taking chances."

"Yea I guess you right, I'm just saying don't set yourself up."

"You're one to talk, TC cheated on you before and you want her. She even cheats now so why are you setting yourself up?"

"Mine and TC's situation is totally different. She was nothing but good to me but I let my insecurities get the best of me. I'm grown now and I know we can have something."

"Well that doesn't justify the fact that she cheated on you before and she's been cheating on a wonderful girl that she has right now."

"I understand that but I have to do this, I haven't stopped thinking about TC since the day I left California and I owe it to myself to see how things would be now."

"Oh ok I feel you, well sis I hope things work out between the two of you. I also hope I get Sam because she really is a good girl and she makes me happy."

"Well sissy I had no idea you were so serious about this girl. I mean if you are happy with her then do what you have to in order to keep her."

"Yea sis at first it was all this little thing you wanted me to do but then after spending time with her and really getting to know her I actually grew feelings. It's crazy because I think I'm falling in love with her."

"Wow well all I can say is; stay positive and let's hope tonight goes as planned."

"Yea it's just going to break my heart seeing Sam in pain after being seen with me by T because I know she loves her and doesn't want to see her hurt. But whatever lets do it."

"You are very right lets get it done. The sooner it's over with the better."

Jay's house

(TC and Jay are getting ready for their date while listening to music.)

"I'm glad I left some clothes here because my ass would have been in queens right now having to come back to the Bronx."

"Yea that is so true, you almost done?"

"Yea you have to move to queens, and yea come on lets be out."

(They both call the girls on the way to the car and tell them to be outside in 5 minutes).

So this is the story of my life I meet great people help them learn to appreciate themselves and they bail on me. Well lets see how tonight goes. Crystal seems real anxious to hang out with me all of a sudden. Well Sam doesn't want me right so at least someone does. I've been having a real bad feeling about tonight; I just hope Jay doesn't get into anything because he can be real jealous. Plus with his insecurities he might think anyone is staring or want to fight everyone.

"T call Crystal and tell her to come outside."

"Ok I got you. Hello Crystal we outside come down."

"Ok boo I'm coming but quick question where we going."

"Good question. Jay where we headed?"

"We're going to Outback in Yonkers."

"Outback's in Yonkers."

"Ok I'll be down in a sec."

"Ok bye."

"Ok jade baby we going to the Outback in Yonkers."

"Ok cool I'm going to call Samantha right now."

"Ok. Thanks sis I love you."

"Yea I love you too Crystal."

(Crystal leaves the house and Jade walks to the back room to where Moe is).

"Yo Moe you not going to ask Crystal where she's going?"

"Nah I don't care man. Honestly I already know what she's up to so I don't even bother."

"So you're saying you not into her like that?"

"I'm not saying that but ever since she found out TC was in NY she's been trying to find ways to contact her but since she knew she had wifey she fell back."

"So how do you feel about all this? Like aren't you going to do anything about it?"

"Well at first I was really upset but I realized I love her enough to see her happy and if getting back with TC is going to make her happy then I'm ok with it. I'm not a dummy though I have a backup plan for when she finally leaves me. Only thing that's going to be tough is this here little boy; I love this kid to death. Hopefully she will let me stay in his life."

"Wow Moe that's deep, I never realized all the people that's involved in getting Crystal back with TC."

"Well Crystal is real selfish so long as she gets what she wants it doesn't matter who she hurts."

"Damn this makes me not want to go through with all this."

"Well I'm not going to tell you what to do but I am going to say that you should think about your happiness. Also there's other ways to get Sam other than making her look like a cheater. When I first met Crystal she was still with her baby's father but instead of trying to mess them up I made us work. She ended up leaving him anyway because I made her much happier."

"You right Moe; I mean she already cut things off between them for me so I'm already in there no need to hurt anyone. I'm not taking Sam there. Thanks Moe I appreciate the talk."

"Anytime little one."

"Hello Sam baby I'm on my way you ready?"

"Yes by the time you get here I'll be waiting outside."

"Oh no babe change of plans I think I want to stay in I got something better planned."

"Really babe I got all dressed up for nothing?"

"Oh it wasn't for nothing trust me."

"Ha-ha ok babe I'll be waiting for you."

(Crystal gets in the backseat with TC and gives her a kiss on the lips. TC raises an eyebrow at Crystal but pays it no mind).

"Crystal you look very nice and you smell good too."

"Thanks you looking good yourself."

"Thank you, thank you very much. Too bad I don't feel as good as I look ha-ha."

"Really you don't feel good what's wrong. If you don't want to go out its fine we don't have to."

"For real we don't awe you're too sweet. Jay take me home."

"What are you serious T?"

"Ha-ha nah man I'm joking I'm good lets go eat I'm starving anyway."

"Awe Tiffany you so silly."

"I try, I try ha-ha."

Man Crystal is really being extra friendly; could she want to be with me? My thing is why? We didn't work when we were together, what makes her think it will work now hmmm I wonder. I wonder what Sam is doing; I miss her extra now ever since she told me she didn't want to be with me I've been thinking about her even more. I don't even know why I'm here

I should be with Sam trying to make up with her, but what if she really don't want that. I would really be wasting my time. I wish I can get into her head for just one day so I can see what she really wants; this is really killing me.

"Tiffany! We're here."

"Oh sorry I was in deep thought."

"Yea I see, hope it was about me."

"Umm yea, come on lets go inside."

"Ewe yea lets do that."

The two couples sit at the furthest table from the door and Crystal keeps looking around when she doesn't see Jade she gives her a call.

"Jade bitch where are you?"

"Crystal sorry I can't do it, but I'm going to talk to you later bye."

"Oh my goodness she's so difficult."

Wow she knows jade too? How ironic is that. Something isn't right here.

"Crystal I'll be right back I'm going to the bathroom."

"Ok."

TC walks toward the bathroom takes out her phone and calls Samantha. When she gets no answer she leaves a message.

"Sam babie when you get this message give me a call I have to talk to you it's very important."

Sam's house (Sam talking to herself)

"I wonder what she wants, should I call her? But what if she's playing games with me? She wouldn't say it was important though. Ugh I'm just going to call."

Sam grabs her phone and calls TC

"Sam babie wassup? What are you doing?"

"I'm home what happen? What is so important that you have to talk to me about?"

"Ok here it goes as a matter of fact can I stop by your house so we can talk?"

"No you can't what happen."

"I really don't want to talk over the phone that's why I want to go over."

"Today isn't good if you want tomorrow you can stop by."

"Hmm ok I guess if that's what's best for you."

"Ok so I see you tomorrow, bye."

"Bye . . . I love you."

"Mmmhmm."

TC hangs up the phone and goes back to the table.

"T you ok?"

"Yea Jay I'm good lets get this over so I can be on my way."

"iight well we all ordered you have to get what you want."

"Ok cool I'll have this right here."

The two couples eat and joke and once everyone is done they go their separate ways, Crystal with TC and Jay with Carly. TC and Crystal walk toward the train and Crystal grabs TC's arm.

"Crystal what is it that you want with me? Things have been over between us for a while so what is it?"

"Ok Tiffany here's the truth ever since I left California I've thought about you. I never forgot about what we had and I miss it, I miss you, I miss us. When I found out you were in NY I knew that was my opportunity to get you back and treat you how you should be treated. I've grown and learned a lot and all that I want to share with you. Tiffany when I first saw you again my heart smiled and I haven't had that feeling in forever."

"Wow Crystal I'm speechless I don't know what to say how to feel. I mean honestly after that first day of seeing you again after so long I did think about you a lot but I didn't think anything of it. I mean I have my wifey and you have whatever it is you have. How can we work where will we start?"

"Well I haven't thought that out but I do know that whatever it takes I'm all for it I'm willing to make things work for us."

"I don't know Crystal things are difficult. I mean maybe we can hang out and see where things go from there."

"Ok Tiffany a slow start I don't mind but let me go I have to get home to my son. You know my number so keep in touch and I'll do the same."

"Ok Crystal get home safe."

TC reaches to give Crystal a hug and when she does Crystal holds her real tight and ends with a kiss. TC notices tears in Crystal's eyes but says nothing she just turns around and walks away.

I don't believe what just happened like for years Crystal was the one for me the only one I wanted and now I'm torn between her and Sam. I mean knowing Crystal wants me back is the best feeling in the world but I'm in-love with Samantha.

Sam's place

"Oh my god jade that was the most beautiful thing someone has ever done for me. Thank you so much baby."

"You are very welcome baby everything was done from the heart and I'm glad you like it. Now lets go to the room for some desert hint hint wink wink."

"Ayy Jade you the best thing that has happened to me. Now come on."

The two make their way to the bedroom kissing each other passionately on the way their way. Jade lays Sam on her back and begins to kiss her all over her body making her moan with pleasure.

"Damn baby you taste so good I can be down there all day."

"Aww T stop."

"What did you just call me?

"Huh, I called you Jade."

"No you called me T; I knew you weren't over her. I have to go."

"Jade baby wait listen, you don't understand I've been with TC for so long she's all that I know."

"It's ok but I'm tired I have to go, I'll see you tomorrow."

"Ok fine Jade goodnight get home safe. Can you at least call me when you get home?"

"Yea I'll call you when I get home, goodnight Samantha."

Jade walks out the door and Sam locks it behind her. Goes into the shower and cries her eyes out.

(Sam thinking) I don't understand what my problem is; I miss my baby so much why am I doing this? What has gotten into me? I have to make things right but Jade oh my god she makes me so happy I'm so confused I hate this feeling. I'm just going to wait till I speak to T tomorrow and see what happens.

Jay's apartment

"It feels so good to be myself around you Jay you don't understand."

"Yea I kind of do understand cause for awhile I wasn't able to be myself either and now that we both know what it is I feel so much more comfortable. I just don't know how I'm going to tell my mom about you."

"Oh baby don't worry yourself about that now let time take its course."

"And the little things you say like this is why I like you so much. Come here and give daddy some sugar."

"Oh yea daddy I'll give you all the sugar you want."

Jay grabs Carly throws her on the bed turns her around and kisses her on her back making his way down to her ass. As he gets closer to the cheeks Carly turns around with her stuff in the air and Jay jumps back.

"Baby what's wrong?"

"I'm sorry baby I just never been in this situation before it's kind of new to me. Umm can you just turn back around I have to get used to this."

"Oh ok babe whatever you want is fine with me."

Jay continues to kiss Carly's back this time wrapping his arms around her to stroke her stuff. Feeling a tad weird Jay continues and hearing the moans takes him to a comfort zone and he opens up completely.

"Wow baby that was incredible. Like an indescribable but great feeling."

"Well I'm glad for that because I've never done things like that before but it felt good I'm so happy I was able to open up the way that I did."

"Me too I'm so happy I give you that comfort. I have to tell you something and it may seem dull but I can't hold it back any longer. I think I'm in-love with you and I know we've only been dating for six months but I knew from the moment I laid my eyes on you that I had to have you."

"Well to keep it real with you I didn't know from day one but chilling with you these past couple of months I've felt something that I haven't felt in a long time. Something really good and I don't want it to stop and this is why I got you a little something. Here it's a promise ring, will you wear it?"

"Oh my god Jay you shouldn't have of course I will wear it. Wow I honestly didn't think you felt the same but now I see you do and this brings joy to my heart. I love you Jay and I want you to know you are the best thing that has happened to me."

"I love you too Carly and I appreciate you coming into my life I just hope you stay for a long time. I'm afraid my mom won't accept this but I honestly don't care because you make me happy and that's all that matters. Plus TC is my best friend and she supports everything about me."

Crystal's house

"Moe?!? I'm home where are you?"

"I'm in the room putting the baby to sleep."

"Hey babe, how was your day?"

"It was pretty good had a lot of QT with the baby. How was your day? You look really happy."

"Oh my day was great I finally I think things are going to go my way after all these years." (As Crystal talks she twirls around with the feeling of excitement and achievement.)

"Well now that you got what you want I have to tell you something. I just don't want what I'm about to tell you to ruin the relationship I have with JR because regardless of anything I see him as mine."

"Oh Moe you know I would never take JR from you, the bond you two have is inseparable. I don't know what he would do without you and I don't want to be the one to mess that up."

"Ok well here it goes . . . ummm I'm seeing someone else and . . ."

"You're doing what?!? Someone else? Who is this other person and for how long? I don't believe you! How could you? I trusted you; I gave you my fucking trust."

"You have some nerve talking about you gave me your trust. Since you found out this TC character was out here you been trying to get to her. Do you think I'm stupid, well I'm not I know what you're up to. I know that once you get this girl where you want her you are going to run with the opportunity so I found someone who makes me happy. And he's pretty great."

"Wait . . . he? What you mean he? You are messing with a guy what kind of dyke are you messing with a dude?"

"I'm tired of you being such a judgmental bitch! Yea I am a dyke but I'm also a female and a human and I fell for someone who treats me good, who shows they care and that's the best feeling. This society is so ridiculous gays want to be accepted but yet if you see two "dykes" together or two "bottoms" together it's a problem or nasty. If a lesbian is with a guy she nasty like how do you judge someone when you don't want to be judged yourself."

"You know what you are a hundred percent right now get your things and get out my house. Maybe this guy can give you a baby because you can forget about mine."

"I'm speechless have a goodnight Crystal."

Moe makes a phone call as she grabs her things and heads out the apartment. Outside she waits for John her new boyfriend.

(Moe thinking) I don't know what just happened that girl is too much going to take little JR from me because I took both of us out of a situation we didn't want to be in. I'm waiting on a guy? This is crazy I don't know if I'm ready for this after being with females for so long. I'm just so tired of going all out for these females and getting nothing in return. I've been with females since I was sixteen and because I am the aggressive one everything is expected from me. Then when I give my all I get played. So I guess giving John a chance isn't a bad idea. I mean he treats me great; he's caring, kind and he appreciates the things I do for him. Well there he is lets see where this experience takes me.

(TC is home laying down thinking about the past couple of months and how things have been going for her.) So much for forever I thought Sam and I would last a life time but I guess stuff like that only happens in books and movies. This is so crazy there is way too much going on for me in a matter of a week I got dumped by my wife my ex who I adored came back into my life and my best friend is finally being himself. Well this is my last chance at getting Sam back so I have to really impress her. (TC grabs her phone to call Sam.)

"Hello Sam don't say anything just hear me out. Ok here it goes from the first day I laid my eyes on you I knew I had to have you. I risked my entire career to be with you and I'm not going to front lately things have been a little rocky but baby I love and I would do anything to get us back. Even if it means moving back to the Bronx so we can be together more."

"Wow TC I'm speechless, I think you should come over here so we can talk in person."

"Oh ok no problem I'll be there in about an hour."

"Ok I'll be waiting."

Well that went pretty good I think things are going to turn out good for me. I got this engagement ring I bought for Sam a few months ago depending on how things go I'm going to give it to her. This means I have to really cut off all the other girls and focus on Sam because I almost lost her and that I cannot bear. (TC gets dress and drives to Sam's house where she sees Jade standing outside.)

"You must be Jade I heard a lot about you. You're Sam's study buddy right?"

"Yea and you must be TC, Sam's ex-girlfriend right?"

"I guess you can say that for now but not for too much longer that's why I'm here."

(TC knocks on Sam's door and Sam opens up.)

(Crystal's apartment)

Crystal talking to herself; I don't believe Moe she cheats and then with a guy like are you serious? Then she going to try and say it's cause I've been chasing TC yea right she probably been talking to that guy. I just hope all this is for the better because Moe was a good girl and if I lose her for nothing that is going to suck badly. I just don't know like if she wasn't good enough to stop me from thinking about TC then maybe she isn't the one after all. Could Tiffany really be my soul mate? It's like whenever I'm with her I feel complete like there are no worries in the world like none what so ever. This life is so confusing but at least I got my baby boy and had Moe, I think I should call her.

"Hello Moe it's me Crystal I'm calling because I think we need to talk so I guess you can call me when you get this message."

No answer damn that sucks she's probably with her boyfriend, this really sucks I don't know what I'm going to do now. Maybe I should call Tiffany but what am I going to say to her like I already told her how I felt and she really didn't seem interested. This is unbelievable I had someone great right in front of my eyes and I let it go for someone who doesn't even know or care to know how I feel for her. What if it was meant for me to chase TC because Moe was going to cheat anyway this is really beginning to annoy me I think I'm just going to stay alone. Wow Moe is calling me back ok, ok.

"Hello?"

"Yea you called me. What happen?"

"Well I said we had to talk but I meant in person so can we meet up somewhere?"

"Umm sure where would you like to meet?"

"Do you mind coming here I have the baby?"

"Yea sure give me a couple hours I'm a little busy right now."

"Ok just call me when you on your way."

"Yeap bye."

"Moe!?"

"What?"

"Never mind I see you when you get here."

"Ok."

Moe hangs up and goes to John's room and begins looking in the draws. Slamming each one as she closes it."

"Moe honey are you ok?"

"Do I look like I'm ok John?!?"

"Alright babe why are you giving me attitude though did I do something to you?"

"Actually you did. You made me fall for you and now I have a girl that I thought I liked and now I'm confused. She wants to talk and I'm sure she's probably going to tell me she wants to be with me but you are here and you treat me so good I don't know what to say how to act how to feel I'm just so confused."

"Well I mean do what you think is best for you whatever makes you happy. I'm not telling you that it would be easy if you leave because it won't but if being with the girl makes you happy then I am happy. I really like you Moe but I also care about your happiness so whatever you decide to do is fine with me."

"You see this is exactly what I mean you say and do the nicest things. You make me feel so comfortable and warm I just don't know anymore. I'm going to take a long walk and think things over, I'll call you later."

"Ok babe be careful out there." (John grabs Moe and gives her a tight hug and a kiss on her cheek)

"Ok John let me go I see you later."

"Alright babe, I love you."

"You would tell me that right now. Bye John."

Moe leaves the house and starts walking up the block talking to herself; "what to do now? Crystal wants to talk to me now and I'm sure it's to get me back but John I'm so happy with him. The thing is I miss Crystal, leaving today made me realize I don't think I can live without her. This entire day she's all I thought about I don't think I can just leave her like this. Moe continues to walk up the block and notices a bunch of girls walking toward her she doesn't think anything of it so she keeps walking. But one of them stops in front of her and asks if she knows John so she answers truthfully and the girls start hitting her. She fights back but as the girls see she is holding her own ground one of them pulls out a blade and slices Moe from her ear to her cheek deeply and another girl hits her on the head with a bottle knocking her out. The ambulance comes but there is no trace of anyone so they take Moe's phone and call Crystal who rushes to the hospital when she hears the news. John finds out about Moe later in the day and rushes down there as soon as he can. When he gets to the hospital he sees Crystal there who is furious and he walks up to her.

"Hello you must me Crystal."

"Yes I am Crystal Moe's wife who is here to take her home. And you are?"

I'm John the reason Moe is here. I am so sorry things happened the way they did. I didn't know my wife was in town."

"Well Mike don't worry you can be on your way I have everything under control. Oh and do me a favor tell your wife this isn't over."

"It's John and please I don't want any trouble. Tell me what I can do to end this safely?"

"John Mike I really don't care and really don't worry, I told you I got everything under control. Good night John."

Sam's house

Sam pauses for a minute then looks at jade.

"Jade what are you doing here?"

"Sam baby I'm tired of all the hiding just tell her so we can be happy together."

"TC baby don't believe her, Jade what are you doing? Have you lost your mind?"

"Sam what is she talking about? What the hell is going on and don't lie to me cause you just going to make things worse."

"TC baby come inside lets talk. Jade please just leave."

"So that's it Sam you just going to throw what we had away all the time we put in, really Sam this is how you going to act?"

"Sam! What the hell is she talking about all this time, you were cheating on me weren't you I knew it. All this shit about being good to you because you are a good girl and this is what you do to me. You know what I'm out of here I hope you are happy now."

"TC baby wait no don't go please I love you baby."

"I'm tired Sam you left me for her right so do you and be happy I just want to go before I say hurtful things."

"Ok TC please can you just call me when you get home, please."

"Goodbye Sam."

"Jade what is your problem?!? How could you do this to me you knew from the start what your place was."

"I'm sorry Sam but I'm falling for you and I'm falling hard. I know TC isn't good enough and doesn't deserve you. I am the one for you."

"Who the hell are you to decide who is good enough and deserves me? I told you in the beginning I love TC she is my heart my everything and now because you want to be a selfish little bitch she's gone and probably won't return."

"I don't believe you just said that what happen to wanting something with me and us being an item huh Sam what about that? You can't keep playing with my feelings and thinking it's ok because it's not all you're doing is damaging me. You are going to make me someone that I'm not without even realizing it. I told you once before lets end it and what did you say? 'Oh no give me some time and all that happen was that my feelings got stronger."

"You are one hundred percent correct I messed up I toyed with your feelings and it wasn't right and for that I am truly sorry but right now I need time to think so if you can just let yourself out I would appreciate it."

"Of course this is what you want. I'm leaving now and there is only one way I'll be back and that's if you are going to be with me out in the open me and you a couple. Other than that don't call, text, email or anything."

"Understandable, I just want to say thank you for coming into my life loving me and treating me as great as you did."

Jade walks out the door waves down a cab thinking to herself. Man what has happen to me this thing went from me trying to cause distance between her and her girlfriend to me catching all kinds of feelings. This is bad any way let me call Crystal and let her know.

"Hello, Crystal all is done. TC is now single hope you are happy."

"As good as that sounds I'm not sure how to feel about it. Moe left me she's seeing a guy. But she's in the hospital right now."

"You don't know how to feel?!?! I just fell for a woman and made her unhappy because she's losing her love and you tell me this? Do you not realize you are messing with people's lives, things were fine the way they were and you ruined it! I'm sorry but I cannot do this anymore I'm done."

"I understand one hundred percent and I don't knock you for being upset. I'm so sorry I hope one day you can forgive me. Thanks for all your help but I have to go."

"Of course you have to go typical of you I hope you get what you deserve. Bye."

Jade sits in the cab wondering what her next step will be. I'm just going to have to move on because I can't do this anymore I have to find happiness and stop interrupting other people's happiness. I'm just so in love with Sam I don't know what to do its killing me. I'm just going to lay low and see what she decides to do.

Samantha is pacing not knowing what it is she should do, she gets on her computer and starts looking through her pictures. She realizes she has way more pictures in her computer with Jade then she does with TC and that majority of her pictures with TC aren't too happy looking. I don't believe I claim TC as my wife, call her my everything, yet I seem so much happier with Jade. Maybe I am supposed to be with Jade and my moving to New York with TC was just a way of getting me to Jade. "Hello?"

"Yea it's TC just want to let you know I'm outside here to get my things. So if you don't mind can you bring them out?"

"TC hey baby you don't want to talk? Any ways give me a minute I'm coming out."

Samantha starts to pack TC things thinking of how she is going to talk to TC and make things up. Ok let me practice what I'm going to say. Babe we have been together for years four to be exact and we cannot let this get between us. I'm not too comfortable with that damn. I guess I'm just gonna let it flow and see how things go. Ok let me go. Samantha walks out the door and TC is in her car with her head down.

"Hey baby I got your things."

(Without picking her head up) "Leave it on the seat I'll get it."

"So you're not even going to talk to me just let all these years go like that."

TC puts her head up her eyes are blood shot red with tears flowing down her face. "I'm letting these years go?!?! If I'm not mistaking you were the one seeing someone else and that isn't even what I'm mad about the fact that you had her at your apartment knowing I can pop up at any time is what gets to me. It's like fuck me you're going to have people at your house and if I see oh well sucks for me."

"T baby can I at least explain? Like do you even want to know how I feel what I've been thinking?"

"You know what go ahead and give me the bull shit excuses of why you had to go and cheat on me. And not just end things."

"You make it sound so harsh but it's understandable you're hurt. Well here it goes when we first moved to NY things were perfect between us we were so happy. Then you got this post office job we moved to different boroughs and everything changed. We don't see one another which I did mention, we hardly talk and it's just like we have a long distance relationship. I don't know about you but for the last three years things have died for me. As far as having her at my place as harsh as this may sound you never did or do pop up at my apartment so I didn't have that scare. What I do want to emphasize is how much I love you and how I wish things can get back or close to how they used to be. I miss you so much and I cry night after night knowing that what we have is dying and there may be no getting it back. I want to be with you forever and I know there is no such thing but in my eyes we can be together for as long as we live. This should be a stepping stone we get over together, I messed up and I know it but cut me some slack I'm human."

"Are you done because I don't have time for this? You cheated so now anything you tell me means nothing at all."

"You act like you're so fucking innocent. I know about all these girls you run around with why the hell do you think I hated you chilling with Jay? But you know what you're right you didn't get caught. At least I can say when you wasn't there Jade was."

"Really that's good to know I have to go." TC drives off crying.

Wow that was really low of her but whatever we're done I refuse to be the one that got cheated on and went back. Let me call Crystal.

"Hey Crystal are you busy?"

"TC? No I'm not wassup?

"Sam and I just broke up she cheated on me and now I don't know what to do. I went to her house and the other girl was there and it all came out."

"Wow TC this is a lot to handle do you want to come over so we can talk?"

"No I can't I'm just going to go home."

"Ok call me when you get there so I know you reached safely."

"Ok bye."

Man I don't know what to do and this ring I spent so much on it like what to do now. Ok let me get myself together ugh this is just too much oh god oh no ahhhhhh.

Crystal is in the hospital with Moe waiting for her to wake out of her coma.

"Moe I'm so sorry I feel like I can take some blame for this if I wasn't chasing after my past and realized what I had in front of my face you wouldn't be here right now. I know one thing when you wake up things will be different I'm going to let you stay in my boys life but I'm afraid I have to let you go."

The nurse enters the room and lets Crystal know she has to go because it is late and if Moe wakes up she will give her a call. Crystal gives Moe a kiss on the forehead and leaves the hospital. Crystal gets on the train and heads home to see Jade there.

"Jade what are you doing why are you packing your clothes?"

"I told you I was done and that comes with me moving out I haven't found a place yet so I can't take all my things but give me until the end of the month and I should be out."

"Jade you are my sister my baby you cannot leave I understand I did you wrong and I played a lot of games but you are the only real person I have aside from my son. If I lose you I will lose myself. You can stay here and not say a word to me but I promised mom and dad I will always be here for you so please don't go."

"Crystal you played with a lot of people's emotions, feelings everything and I don't know how I can stomach being around you not knowing if you will try to pull something like this off again."

"Jade I can give you my word that I would not and I will even tell TC the truth about everything and clear your name."

"Ok I guess I can stay. I love my sister too much to leave her side come give me a hug."

The two hug and Crystal gets a phone call.

"Hello? TC oh my god no. what happen? Oh ok I'm on my way. Jade TC was in a big car accident can you give me a ride to the hospital?"

"Sure, what happened though is she ok?"

"I'm not sure they said she was hit by a truck crazy thing is I spoke to her earlier about her break up and she seemed bothered but I didn't think it was that bad."

"Damn that's crazy I hope she's ok though I mean I don't wish that on anyone." (I wonder if Sam knows, wait that isn't my place.)

"Wait I have a number for her best friend I can call him so that he can go too. Hello Jay it's Crystal TC's friend I just got a call from the hospital she was in a car accident so you might want to go I'm on my way there now."

Jay's house

Man I don't believe I just got a phone call like this my fucking best friend hospitalized and I can't get in contact with Susan. Well let me call her one last time and get out of here. 'Susan baby I've been calling you but no answer so I guess you can give me a call when you get a chance. I'm going to the hospital for TC anyway I love you talk to you later.' Ok got that call out the way now to call Sam I'm sure she would like to know what's going on. 'Hello Sam it's Jay I just received a called that TC is in the hospital she was in an accident. Ok see you there.'

Hospital, TC's room

"Oh my god Jade do you see her she looks horrible, TC?"

"Crystal she can't hear you she's un-conscious."

Samantha hurries in TC's room seeing Crystal and Jade there already.

"Crystal? What are you doing here? And Jade you too? What's going on here?"

"Well you must be Samantha TC's ex don't worry she's in good hands now my sister Jade and I will take care of her."

"Jade? What's going on how do you know Crystal?"

"I guess you didn't hear me when I said she was my sister. And as far as you and TC go you guys are over we are going to try and work things out hence why I got a call before you."

"Crystal there you go again this is what I mean about you man. Samantha this is my sister and she talked me into trying to get with you so you and TC could build distance but in the process I fell for you."

"So all this was just a game to get me out of TC's life huh well I wish you the best with her and jade . . . I have no words for you what so ever I'm out of here."

Samantha runs out and Jay walks in confused to what was going on.

"Sam where are you going?"

"I bet you had something to do with all this also, let me go!"

"Hey you 2 thanks for the call, what's the deal with her?"

"She'll be ok; glad you can make it now we can go I'm sure you can take things from here."

"You're leaving so soon I mean its all good just asking."

"Yea well my girlfriend got jumped over some John guy from 138 and willis, his wife and her friends or something like that so I have to be sure she's ok."

"John? Girl I'm dating used to see a John from over there. How you know that's where he's from?

"that's where Moe was found and she was over his house."

"Hmm well I can do some research for you if you want maybe find out who his wife is."

"Oh yea that would be great, where the hell is my sister I'm ready to go home now."

Jade is running after Samantha calling her name

"Sam, Samantha hold on please."

"What is it Jade? What kind of fool would you like to make of me now?"

"Listen I've been wanting to tell you about this for a long time and I'm so sorry we had to become an item under these circumstances but I mean you can't say there isn't a part of you that feels we are meant to be."

"Oh yes the hell I can because if it wasn't for your manipulative ways we probably wont even know one another. This is the last thing I expected from you and what sucks is I actually had feelings for you and was going to tell TC I couldn't be with her so I can be with you so as bad as I feel about this accident it showed me true colors. I don't want to see you again have a wonderful life."

"Dammit! Sam please don't do this I need you in my life I love you woman don't you see this?"

"I'm sorry I have to go now Jade."

Sam walks away tears flowing from her face thinking to herself. 'This is crazy first I lost my love which isn't really that bad because if someone was able to change how I feel about her then that's an issue. I never ever would have expected that from jade and to think I was really falling for her and trusted her. I would never trust another person again.'

Jade walks back to the hospital gets Crystal and without a word drove back home.

"So I'm guessing you're done with me?"

"Should I not be once again you lied and screwed me over! I lost the woman that I love because of you, but you know what girls come and go family doesn't so as done with you as I am I'm not going anywhere. Just one thing keep me the hell out of your vicious ways!"

"Most definitely, don't worry about that; no more games for me promise."

Jay is in his car on 138 and Willis Avenue waiting around to see if he possibly sees John. To his surprise not only does he see John but he also sees Carly who is with him. Not knowing what to do Jay stays in the car but calls Carly.

"Of course no answer and she looked at the phone so there's no excuse. I'm running out of patients with this girl. What the fuck she's kissing this nigga seriously."

Jay gets out the car and walks in Carly's direction.

"So this is your reason for not answering my phone calls? You're too busy with your so called stalker ex?"

"OMG Jay what are you doing here and I've been meaning to call you I was just busy."

"What am I doing here what the fuck are you doing here I've been calling you back to back my best friend is in the hospital and her ex's girlfriend got jumped. The reason I'm here is simply because my best friend's ex's girl got jumped over some John guy from 138 and Willis so I assumed it was this dude. I came to see if I can find out who his wife is now since I couldn't contact you but I got it all figured out it was you. Does he know you're a man too or did you trick him also? I'm fucking done with you!"

"Listen Jay I don't know you but I sure don't need you spying on me or sitting outside my house."

"Check it out homeboy you don't know me not one bit so don't come at me saying what you need or don't need got it? This is between me and this fucking slut over here."

"Jay! . . ."

"Carly baby I got this."

John hooks Jay and Jay looks at John startled. "Are you serious homeboy? You have to come better than that. (Jay jabs John twice followed by a hook knocking him out). You see this Carly you bought the worse out of me and to think I was ready to introduce you to my family not caring what they thought. There really isn't anyone in this world I can trust. I do appreciate you making me feel comfortable in my own skin."

"Jay baby I'm so sorry I didn't think you liked me this much. I thought you were ashamed of me I didn't realize I'm so sorry."

"So all the phone calls, me being around, doing nice things for you did all that mean nothing to you? I went out of my way to keep you happy and this is the thanks I get? Maybe if you weren't busy chasing your ex we would have worked. I feel sorry for you, I have to go farewell."

"OH Jay please give me another chance to show you I am all about you."

"I'm sorry but you had your chance I'm not one for getting played and giving a second chance. I called you back to back to back you know why because my damn best friend is in the hospital but you were too busy jumping people over some dude."

Jay walks to his car driving off to the hospital to see TC. On the way he calls Crystal to tell her about John's wife.

"Hello Crystal I know John's wife if you meet me at the hospital I can give you a picture of her."

Jay gets to the hospital and TC is still unconscious. He sits at the side of her bed and starts talking to her.

"TC baby I'm so sorry you are in this situation I promise when you get up I will care for you and not let anything happen to you. It's me and you against the world people these days cannot be trusted I have so much to tell you."

"Jay?"

"Crystal hey I got that picture for you, here that's her well not really her that's a man but yea you can find her right around where John lives that's where they're hanging out."

"OMG thank you so much but did you say guy? Why are you . . . you know what never mind I'm going to get going."

As soon as Crystal walks out TC wakes up and calls out for Jay.

"T OMG your awake how are you feeling?"

"UMMM I honestly don't know right now, what's going on?"

"You were in a terrible car accident a truck hit you."

"This is horrible what about work how will I work will I be ok?"

"Well you had a really bad head injury and your legs got caught so you would need therapy to walk properly again."

"This isn't good no this can't be how will I pay my bills? No no no I can't, get me out of here." TC tries pulling the wires off and Jay gives her a soothing hug.

"T baby relax you have me, you have a huge law suit coming because the truck was a company and the guy ran the red light. In the mean time you are going to move in with me as far as working for the post office you have to give that up. I've been working on your resume to find jobs in education now that you're awake you can actually go on interviews."

"Wow Jay all this for me but what happen to Samantha and Crystal?"

"Well I'm not too sure what happen with Sam I know when I found out I called her to let her know. Crystal is the one that called me when I got to the hospital I overheard Sam and Crystal talking. Crystal said you two were an item now and that since you and Sam broke up she can go on with her life. The thing is there was a Jade girl here too and she told Sam that Crystal convinced her to come between you and Sam so she can have you. When I walked in Sam was so upset she left Crystal stood but a little while after she left also. She told me her girlfriend got jumped over some John guy who happened to be Carly's ex. I went to see if I possibly saw them because Carly was acting very different not answering my calls or text. I ended up seeing them together so now it's over between Carly and I."

"Well damn how long have I been unconscious for all this to happen? I remember Sam and I breaking up she played me I can't be with her and I understand she was manipulated but she got completely out of hand with it. As far as Crystal goes I cannot associate with someone that will do anything possible to have me even if it includes ruining my relationship. Now that we are both single I guess we can concentrate on ourselves right. I am so glad to have you as a best friend come give me a hug."

Jay leans in to hug TC and at the same time he kisses her and to his surprise she kisses him back.

"TC I have to tell you something and I hope this doesn't ruin our relationship."

"Man the fact that you're by my bed right now means a lot I doubt whatever it is you have to say can ruin anything between us."

"Well the truth is I'm in love with you. I mean your style your swag everything about you. I want to be with you."

"I love you too."